Anwar,
the Very Bright Meerkat

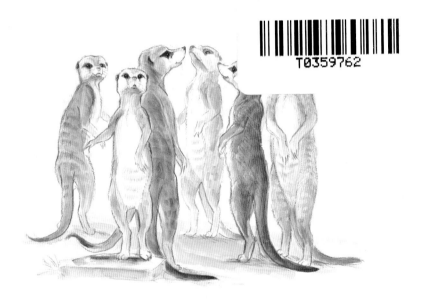

Written by Patrick Lay

Illustrated by Meredith Thomas

Flying Start
to Literacy®

Contents

Chapter 1:
The new pups

Once, a mob of meerkats lived in the desert in Africa.

One day, four new pups were born.
Three of the pups looked just like all the other meerkats, but one pup looked different.
His name was Anwar and his fur was bright red with golden stripes.

Nia, the oldest and wisest meerkat in the mob, held Anwar in her arms.

"You are different," she said, "but you will find your place."

Anwar and the pups grew quickly.
They spent their days playing with each
other and exploring.

The days and weeks passed. Soon, the pups
were ready to help the mob hunt for food.

"Tomorrow, you can help us dig for food,"
said Zula, the leader of the mob.
"But you must be careful. It is dangerous
work. When we are digging, our heads are
down and our tails are up. We can't see
who might be coming to eat us!"

But Anwar wasn't scared. This was the day
he had been waiting for!

Chapter 2:
A lucky escape

Early the next morning, Anwar and the mob were busy digging for food.

With their heads down and their tails up, the meerkats did not know that Jackal was also out looking for food. He was looking for his favourite food – meerkats!

At first, Jackal couldn't
see the meerkats because
they were the same colour
as the sand. But then
Jackal saw Anwar's bright
fur. He began to
creep towards Anwar.

Anwar's head was down in the sand and his tail was up. He didn't see Jackal creeping closer and closer.

Just at that moment, Zula looked up from her digging and saw Jackal.

"Run," she called. "Run quickly! Jackal is coming! Down the bolthole! Quick! Quick! Quick!"

All the meerkats ran as fast as they could
to the safety of their bolthole.
Anwar ran to the bolthole too, just as
Jackal was about to strike!

Chapter 3:
No job for Anwar

The next day, before the mob went out to dig for food, Zula said to Anwar: "You cannot come digging with us today."

"Why not?" asked Anwar.

"Because you are too easy for Jackal to see," said Zula. "Your fur is too bright and it puts us in danger."

Anwar was very upset. He tried hard not
to cry. He turned and walked away.
When he was far from the rest of the mob,
he cried and cried.

But Anwar wasn't alone.

Nia, the oldest and wisest meerkat, had followed Anwar. She wanted to help him.

"Don't be upset," she said. "You are different, but you will find a way to help the mob."

"You're wrong," said Anwar. "How can I ever help my mob with this bright coat of mine?"

"You are part of our mob," said Nia. "You just have to find your place."

Chapter 4:
Anwar's last chance

The next day, when the mob went out to dig for food, Anwar was left behind again.

As he stood by the bolthole and watched them go, he kept thinking about what Nia had said:

You are part of our mob.

You just have to find your place.

Soon, the mob was out of sight. Anwar
stretched his neck up, but he couldn't see
the mob.

He jumped up and down, but he still
couldn't see the mob.

Then he stood up on his tippy toes.

Suddenly, Anwar could see everything!
He could see Nia, with her head down and
tail up, digging for food.

He could see all of his brothers and sisters,
heads down, tails up, digging for food.

And he could see Jackal creep, creep, creeping closer and closer towards the mob.

"Run!" screamed Anwar. "Run, quickly! Jackal is coming!"

The mob looked up.

"Anwar is right," yelled Zula. "Run quickly! Run for your lives!"

All the mob ran as fast as they could back to the bolthole. They kicked up the dust behind them as they ran.

Anwar stayed standing tall, watching Jackal until all of his family was safe.

Back in the burrow, the meerkats gathered around Anwar.

"Thank you, Anwar," said Zula.
"You saved us!"

Nia looked at Anwar with her wise, old eyes.

"How did you know Jackal was nearby?" she asked.

"I saw him," said Anwar.

"But how could you see him?" asked Nia.

"I stood up tall on my back legs," said
Anwar. "And I could see all around.
I could see everything. And that was
how I saw Jackal."

"You must show us how," said Nia.

And so it was that Anwar became the first meerkat to stand on guard duty. He taught the other meerkats how to stand tall on their hind legs. He taught them how to look out for danger and keep the mob safe.

"I knew you were different," said Nia. "And now you have found your place in the mob."